What Othe
Paying for ~~Gas with~~ *Quarters*

"War, family, life, and death collide in this collection. Allen's reverberating lines beat with ear-splitting blasts of beauty."

—Jason Poudrier, author of *Red Fields*

❖ ❖ ❖

"'No / matter the changes / they never feel / correct' (from "Sometimes a Poem'). The odyssey of Aly Allen's *Paying for Gas with Quarters* takes the reader through the trials of parenthood, adult relationships, a military career, transitioning into civilian life, and discovering self-identity through it all. Her debut collection challenges memory and the present to hold beauty and pain together in one vision, just like a field of poppies blooming in a field to honor what was lost and what should be celebrated."

—Lisa Stice,
author of *FORCES*, *Permanent Change of Station,*
and other poetry collections

❖ ❖ ❖

"Aly Allen's words awaken us to the parallels of military and war to parenthood. The messy, entangled chaos that is inevitably life-changing. She is unafraid to reveal her human-ness through these poems, the places where 'I-am' becomes where 'I-am-lost.' *Paying for Gas with Quarters* weaves together complex truths: War changes us and yet leaves us longing, still, for connection."

—Jessi M. Atherton,
author of *The Time War Takes: Poems*

"In *Paying for Gas with Quarters*, Aly Allen weaves the chaos of war into the fabric of parenthood. Her poems crash like mortar fire over the reader in staccato bursts of heart-wrenching emotion. She finds commonalities between the everyday isolation of parenting, and the 'composed vibrations' of battle. This collection is at once a quiet elegy and a defiant war cry that reminds readers how fragile—and valuable—life is."

—Gary Reddin,
author of *An Abridged History of American Violence*
and *Quantum Entanglement*

"New war voices bring new war stories! Aly Allen's clear-eyed poems of battle are tinged with humor and hope. Regardless of their own circumstances, geographies, and life-experiences, readers will surely be comforted with this revelation: We are all in this together. We are each deserving of grace."

—Randy Brown,
author of *Welcome to FOB Haiku*

Paying for Gas
with Quarters

Poems

Aly Allen

Middle West Press LLC
Johnston, Iowa

Caleb,
I cannot wait for your poems to come out!

Aly Allen

Poetry / Global War on Terror / Trauma & Healing

Paying for Gas with Quarters
by Aly Allen

ISBN (print): 978-1-953665-22-5
ISBN (e-book): 978-1-953665-23-2
Library of Congress Control Number: 2023937533

Middle West Press LLC
P.O. Box 1153
Johnston, Iowa 50131-9420
www.middlewestpress.com

Special thanks to James Burns of Colorado Springs, Colorado and Nathan Didier of Cedar Falls, Iowa!

Your patronage helps publish great military-themed writing!
www.aimingcircle.com

To my kids

To all families
absorbing wounds they never sought

To all my siblings

CONTENTS

Hero Worship

Underworld

Don't Thank me for my Service

I joined the military
Because I wanted to die.
I was too scared to really
Try. Drinking and reckless abandon
Under the guise of service.
I even get goodwill for this.

No. I have not earned it yet.
Swore to protect from threats foreign
And domestic. In America, the oppressed
Face daily threats. Drag queens teach
Children literacy and love, while hate groups
Openly threaten their lives and protest.
What is being done about all the terrorist
Walking our streets? They cover their faces
And call for freedom, but only for themselves.
They protest with weapons when told to
Cover their mouth to protect their neighbor.
Angry, white, man with a gun is an expectation
Not a profile of a threat. The textbook says so.
Why is the National Guard not protecting
Black people from the police? We have unseated
Regimes, families, dynasties, for statistically less.

I did not battle anyone during deployment.
Gave pens to paperless schoolchildren.
Got shot at on patrol, sure that is expected
As the shield. We did not have anyone
Hiding behind us though. We admonish the Taliban,
Their oppression of women,
Claim their country

3

Backwards, in need of help.
We shout to deflect.
Not so much a flake
As a snowstorm. I wander
Off into the drift. The winter
Slows both insurgencies.

Gunfire in the alley,
I charge and start to round the corner,
Withheld by the platoon sergeant,
My chances poof into dirt walls.

The story goes, I joined
To serve like my grandpas,
To travel the world.
Even I believed it for an odyssey.
The incoming artillery siren
Wails. I saunter to the bunker.
Don my armor once inside it. Joke
With fellow soldiers about the obscene,
Absurd, obscure. Anything to elicit,
Overwhelm any possibility of exploding.
After ten minutes a soldier sleeps
Beside me. It sounds as if he gargles
Yogurt. It dulls the whistle overhead.
The conductor calling all aboard.
Death departs from spontaneous stations
Everywhere we go. I switch my rifle off safe
Fire twenty-one shots into the sky.
The other soldiers nod.

Communal complicity relieves
A smidge of guilt. I am
Glad I did not die in Afghanistan.

I worry now for the lives it would have cost.
The medics rushed to meet the dead,
The dying. They check for tickets,
Unload bags. They unhook one car,
Lighten the load. The train pulls out,
Picks up speed. I chase
Until my muscles give. No,
I survived. I did not earn anything more.

Why does the flag wave

in the wind. Demanding my attention.
Reminding me of them. Of when
they didn't show up for
final formation. When everyone paid
their respects, stories were
told. A legend was born.
The green berets dropped
their covers at the foot
of his battlefield cross.
They knew better than us

how to establish fear. Spread it
democratically. There isn't a price
we wouldn't pay! Why did they
pay and I didn't? The flag
rolls like time   folds   flaps
flutters before me.   I drape myself
beneath, breathe the fabric,
inhale, attempting to asphyxiate.
The cloth smothers, but air leaks
through. The esophagus fuses
with the fibers. Now I am flapping,
the stripes inescapable.

Culpability

The color pops on the inside,
coated by draping red petals.
The purple pours forth, protrudes.
Every year the field
is awash in the memory of blood,
blossoming, bursting out—a life
cycled to celebrate, a sacrifice—
overflowing with seeds of the sown.
Wine-dark Sea carried

by generations yet to pass.
More required each successive
year, for the soldiers slain by mines, machines,
others, and the self. Flowers flank
the heartbeat. Pulse. Roots run

shallow, a pool of new sustenance
seasonally. The patch spreads,
pollinates even the least populous
swaths of earth. Weeds which reseed
themselves. The poppy makes a new neighbor.

ALY ALLEN

There Won't be any Veterans

committing suicide if there are

no veterans. Not extermination

of the current. Elimination of

the future. No service. No

obligation. No ultimate sacrifice. No

unpayable debt. Survivor's guilt

gone. Moral wounds

gone. Unscarred. Disbanding

the military could prevent

depression, and think of all

the civilians who won't be

casualties. The condolences

and monuments we won't

have to craft. And,

if there are not veterans,

perhaps also, there will

be only a memory,

a well-rehearsed verse

about ancestors and war.

Tinnitus

Starts with a bubble over
my ear. Like a sound barrier

muffling the outside din,
while within the building

begins. Unleashing, like
it was loaded. Aimed. Directed

directly in. Bludgeoning every
percussive surface between

both drums. The sound
has always tried to escape.

The bubble, the barrier,
is the pain of holding it in.

From Behind Me

The hollow wave of a one-year-old
skull bouncing off fabricated wood.
My socks shuffle across carpet, churning,
charging. Does he need an injection?
How long would the ambulance take?
Would they Life Flight him to Tulsa or OKC?

Helicopters travel across Adirondack mountains, simulating
our movement in Afghanistan. The pilot,
reminds us that I.E.D.s don't hit helicopters.

I'm in the room with the echo. Please be screaming
more from the shock than from the pain.
His sister hides from blame behind a pile
of stuffed animals. Don't be a concussion,
don't be unconscious, be conscious,
let it be nothing but an abrasion.

Black Hawks: composed of vibrations and a spinning sort of pound,
most call it a whirl, but it's more of a slap really.
I can't call the rides silent, static might be more accurate,
not quite right, not quiet for certain.
The landing is a high-pitched dive into a wallop.

I check his whole head twice,
feeling for something to undent.
An elephant apologizes in his sister's voice.
I poach the pachyderm with a rant
about safety, about the imminence of death.

Battle Buddy

I'm not a helicopter parent,
I do contextualize

everything through narration,
I'm not sure I've introduced myself

except through what I imagine
my children would have to say.

I'm no longer sure which thoughts
are internal. My son keeps pulling

The *Iliad* off the shelf. I've started reading
random passages aloud, to slow

the emptying. I thought myself Achilles,
once, until I discovered his rage. Now I know.

I am no demigod.
Fear felt useful during deployment. Time

was what we had too much of. At home,
I have an abundance of fear, and no time

to organize it. Sleep is when I'm meanest.
The blood wipes out of the fridge, though
the jelly is starting to seem permanent.
I make my son a gluten-free PB&J

every day. He doesn't wake up
screaming any longer. The pandemic feels

a lot like deployment. Invisible enemy,
limited mobility, civilian casualties, racist excuses

for violence. At least in Afghanistan
the oppression is out in the open. I can't yell

around my 11-month-old. Not at
the TV. Not at anyone. Not about

anything. I shouldn't yell. Now
I can't. He always starts crying. Why

didn't I feel bad before?
He runs like I breathe. To breathe

it seems. Jumping kickstarts his joy.
He won't sit still. Won't is perhaps

my perception. My need not his.
His sister wants her pants back. He's still

flapping a leg in each hand. He wants.
I want. I plan.

He disarms me in the moment,
drags me around the field twice.

Tinnitus

A piercing, a funneling
of pressure, a resonate rolling

cone, the building of a wave
not the crashing of a wall.
It's almost a full minute
before I realize the tornado

siren is blaring. The sun is shining
& my ears are not ringing.
Piercing touches on the senses,
the senses ringing neglects.

I don't hear the piercing
as much as I feel it.
It's not a vibration.
I hear warnings, foreshadowing sampled
one note at a time. I saw it
in a picture once, on the wall,
at the VA hospital, image of a jet
breaking the sound-barrier,
a breath-like cone of cloud.
Those clouds I could hear.

Sometimes I escape,
twist my neck
against my shoulder. Strain
the pressure,
coil the piercing,
load it like a spring for later.

I think about the fact that I'll never hear
that exact tone again. The tone
exited existence. I dread
the recoil, spend more time
lamenting the pitch and its leaving.

Roll Call

The surface of the pool ripples—white lines
across chlorine blue. Dust blows
Afghan dust kicks, plumes, never settles,
eighty worn, rubber boot-heels clap.

through the air, crystallizes into water.
Newborn in my arms, older sister not visible.
The dust is inside my uniform more than on it.
Another memorial begins:
"Roll call!"

Two-year-old kicks aren't hard enough to crack the surface.
I'm standing on the deck. She is still
underwater. Her eyes bulge for the surface.
"Private Fernandez?"
"Here, First Sergeant!"

Please! Please. Just one more bubble.
"Specialist Brown?"
"Here, First Sergeant!"

I fling her from the pool to her mother. I'm still.
"Sergeant Anderson?"
She coughs water onto the deck.

"Sergeant Benjamin Anderson?"
She folds over her mother. I can't hear their tears.

"Sergeant Benjamin T. Anderson?"
over the tinnitus. I see them heaving,

Taps.
Sobbing, breathing, and look down at my son,
who splashes the water and begs to stay in.

Restless Leg Syndrome

The dream is always
The same. Even in different places—
The chase through sludge. Pursuit?
      Why am I running ... is that ... wait!
The more frequent the steps
The shorter the distance
Between them. The child is out of reach—
The peripheral blur—accelerates
The feeling.
I'm not moving.
The need to move.
The inability to reach

Them.   The separation spreads
The silhouette is what I seek,
Landscape's shadow submerging with horizon
Unnatural shapes in squandered light
Sunset starts the race

Heavy legs	syrup fields
So, so	much seeking
Silenced	screaming
Extended	hallways
Looping	cut scenes
Unseen	lurking
Pursued by	feeling
I can't keep	up
Three strides	from where
They float	like thought

Listen Up Kids,

Step 1:   be   noiseless
Step 2: run!
Step 3:
                              (hide)
Step 4: FIGHT

run   hide   fight
hide   fight   run
fight   run   hide

Run to classrooms with barricaded doors.
Flee from an alligator, or crocodile, whichever
the children find more fun.
Straight lines draw the eye of the shooter.

The best way to survive is _____.
When you are present, keep calm.
Tell everyone else to remain
calm. Exude calmness.

Be alert.   You are much
less likely to be shot
if we pull the trigger first. Hope
he entered the other end of school.
Emily covers her mouth. Almost
doesn't start to cry.
The teacher pulls out a basket of pistols—
a few kids faint—
passes them out.
Older students arm younger.

Everyone is a threat.

Someone shouts *The floor is lava,*

all of the children unload
their weapons. Bullets fight off
fear. No need to be afraid
when the gun is unloaded.
Debrief your classes
following an active shooter. Younger children
want a one- maybe two-sentence story. Simply
replace the Fourth Graders' memories.
Ask the remaining teenagers what they will do
next time it happens.

I stepped on Legos to Prepare for this Poem: A Triptych

I.

Try and remain atop the blocks
For the duration of oration.

II.

I'm trying to teach
My eldest how to control
My anger. Rather, I'm demanding
They figure out how
How I am to regulate
Myself or any other sixteen
Paces. Trace your spaces.
I know what you are.

III.

Like a drill sergeant
Enters my apartment
Wipes finger
Across the residue

ALY ALLEN

Daddy why are

you not
mad at
me   you

usually get
mad at
me when
my spill
you yell

Keep Putting the Baby-Gate Back up

To bar myself in the kitchen.
Keep the kids in sight.

They keep climbing over
when my back is turned.

They sneak to the trash,
empty the bin. Spread

waste across tiles. Stack
spills for me to clean

in the corner. I return them
to the living room. Secure

the gate, return to cooking.
They bull rush it together

knock it all the way down.
I close the drawers

forget where the silverware is. Turn
the oven off and subsist on cereal.

Nocturnal Lactose Intolerance

Uncle Roger was a United
States Marine. Found out
after he died. Though,
he did always sport
the high-and-tight haircut,
his movies were organized

meticulously, his bed made.
I remember him drinking
milk, just like a friend
who killed himself upon
our return from deployment.

When my grandparents
visited, one night Roger got up
late, for his usual midnight
milk, instead, took his handgun

shot himself at the desk.
The noise woke his wife,
my Mamaw, Papaw. I think

Uncle Roger was already seated,
sipping in Valhalla with my friends.

As the sun sets, I pour milk out.

Tinnitus

An unending
noise. Scraping,
piercing pipes.
Pulling apart
ear drum. Hum.

Lock jaw
for centuries seeking
to unappear for always.

Battlefields

Plead for me Thetis

I fear my daughter
will inherit the feuds of Achilles.
I beg your guidance,
Pleading Thetis, you stayed your son from battle,
bestowed gifts of Hephaestus, and your favors
with the nod of Zeus. Once,
you saved the blacksmith,
your son you could not.

Shouts hang in her closet.
I've injected anger in her veins—
She'll suffer fits of menis.
Prophecy hasn't scribed her destiny,
she'll scale Ilion walls someday.
My daughter is no demigod,
yet paths to Olympus persist.

Grant her, Nereid,
the same divine armor,
donned by the King of Myrmidons,
though steer her from conflict—
sharply, with words of wisdom and myths
of monsters, immortals, and men—
spare them her ferocity—
she'd drag them in circles—
spare them Priam's grief.
Grant her, Shapeshifter,
the power to reassign the apple,
may she only pass her anger onto her enemies.

Tinnitus

Often an echo,
               something
reminiscent.
              Scents set

off the sentimental siren.
                    Affectionately
shielding me, erasing memories,
                       moments of
nostalgia, recalled within a cyclone.

                         Alone, spinning
around, while rotating and also
                  orbiting,
A party of destruction.

Fort Drum, 2008

Riva Ridge is a loop. It surrounds
Korengal Valley Boulevard and is crossed
by Euphrates. The base handbook says
until 30-below we must perform
all physical conditioning outdoors—every degree
below Zero better preparation. The Adirondacks
running up to Appalachian,
a stand-in for the Hindu Kush, mountains
more like foothills next to Himalayan giants.

Orders come from the 3-foot footprints
in front of me. Abominable upstate tundra
removes everything except resilience. Insulated
uniforms, conceal out-of-regulation
Under Armour, layers built to sustain arctic licks.

The formation keeps falling.
Tracks are filled with snow before they are found.
The only identifiable direction is down.
The Black River is frozen solid.

My mind skates downstream
to Sackett's Harbor Brewing Co.
a pint fills my balaclava with froth.

Everything stiffens   to endure
the frigid nature of lake-effect snow.

Shivers are a sign of life. Lake
Ontario supplies the blizzard's breath.
Soft powder soaks up echoes, whispers

appear puffs, whisps, whipped

over barrack's rooftops. Shouts
flurry into snow drifts. Flakes
crackle. Frost waves. The sun's rays bound
from crystals on the ground, engulf

the eyes with bright.
Knee-deep strides,
each a minute. Against
the burning cold, accumulating. Snot
creeps into my throat, tasteless.

Recall

I don't wear camouflage anymore,

not because it keeps civilians from seeing   me,

but because

       they already can't.

I'm imitating their perception,
Or perhaps I'm—   projecting.
The crazy mumbling veteran.   Proselytizing
nonsense.
Drinking liquor from a bag, holding my hand out.   Proffering
nothing.
They make bets predicting my suicide.

The projectiles still wake me
      at night, at least

The soft rumble of a rocket exploding nearby
gently sways me from sleep.
The whistle of its comrade jars me awake
before the air raid sirens scream,
we scurry to the bunker,

                  the memory of us.

It's not smoke exactly,
rather   cooked dirt.
Flash-fried to the perfect temperature.
The sulfur hesitates after someone strikes a match.

ALY ALLEN

I don't wake up in the bunker

                                    And I never sleep
inside it.

Portrait in Apocalypse

Deep-fried by the Texas Sun,
my skin boils more than it burns.
I say howdy and I don't much know
any strangers. From around the corner,
my baritone projects the image
of a much taller man. I wonder,
will they recognize me?
While the cows remain in pen
the grass in the pasture grows.
They isolate themselves until
released. The field they gather in delivers
a sermon, each blade of grass
a preacher, prophesying sustenance.
Scotch burns, swells my belly into a barrel.
My first drink is always after last-call. Before
my barstool spins around the sun
I'll pen the perfect painting.
I prefer to write on parchment
which is being pulled into a paper shredder.
The green blades pass through their
seven stomachs before being decomposed, deconstructed,
combined into a plaster—
the cow dung which calls forth
the descendants of the field.
I always take two scoops of ice cream.
Whatever flavor we have
in the freezer is my favorite.
Fun is the only abstraction
I feel I ever earn. I wonder,
from what pasture does my pint originate?
Instead of brain-freeze

I get chest-chills, when eating spoonfuls
too fast. I always empty the carton.

Road Trip

Instead of speaking to the passenger
I turn the radio up. Riding waves across
the world on repeated notes.

En route to the airport—
another temporary destination—
I drop them off but keep their baggage.

Instead of switching lanes
I impede faster traffic. Watching them wave
as they swerve around to the right

on Route 66—where once upon a time families
travelled for vacation—historical markers,
already cemeteries, flicker in various neon.

Instead of slowing down for the lights
I accelerate away. They follow, multiply,
make me feel wanted, spread like

feeders for the highway. Rattling across
imagined borders, they tail me from state
to state. Fuming I stop.

ALY ALLEN

An Unexpected Blast

I start to feel
unsafe. A roadside
box. *SLAP*
CRASH Sound
rolls, splashes, surrounds

screams. Then, I hear my voice
cursing the cars around
me. The horns are at
fault. The brake lights
they spite me.
All the other drivers
know which lane
I need. I know
they impede intentionally.

I calculate the cost of new
fenders before realizing
there is no bomb,
only an explosion.

Guard Tower

Assignment: Search Team, Front gate
    There is trust here. It
    Is broken. We question them
                          Search them
    In their homeland. *on

               Sarge says, *Suspect them all. They are waiting*
               For us to relax. The morning we do is the morning
               They storm. The explosives are what you cannot
               See. Searching for them provides security.

Assignment: Turret Gunner, Humvee outside front gate
                                Five-second bursts
-    Watch Perseid meteor shower through night vision goggles
    Green   sky   streaked,   absent
Incoming   fire   whistles,   chirps,
    flutters,
    Galaxies   swirl within.   Shower
    the sky

With   centuries.   Sustain those   staring
             At the moon.   Hypnotized,
    searching
    For the stars   comprising
    Virgo.
Something   rising,
           Not my anxiety.
    Aware of every   star,   every milky   crevice. Eons

Glimmer   merely moments.   I   can't
    Remember   to glance   at the
road.

        I hope   the soldier   in   the
driver's seat
Isn't looking   up.   I'm   glad   I
   set
   A   timer   to   change
      The barrel   of
the 50-cal.

Assignment: Local National Workers Escort, On Base

Like a hawk, nah, an eagle

-     Question any need for the rifle
around my neck. The strap
a worm in my Adam's apple.

Assignment: Watchman, Guard Tower

It stinks here, this country.

-     Monitor the burn pit
-     Inhale fumes from burning:

                 rubber, rust, hard drives,
                    secrets, shit, toxic rot.

-     There are rifle mounts on either front corner
              of the exterior walkway. I'm told
                it's adorned on all sides
       with bulletproof glass. Occasionally, I mount my M-4
          on the outside. Mostly, I hide from the odor.
        Afghanistan stinks because of what we bring
                     & burn.

Threats are to be simultaneously shot and reported.

- The main entrance is a gauntlet
- It shoots straight out from the guard tower
- The tower is the last line of defense,
                    aside from the hundreds of armed
              men and women, sleeping and working beyond.
- There are hills on every side but South. I face
                  North. None of the hills are overwhelming,
                            though all of them conceal.

The shards   slap   back   of   neck
a moment
after   hearing   shatter. I   hit the   floor.
      Kevlar
      beside   the radio.   Hands   at neck,
      preparing,
plugging   wound,   pushing   blood   within.
      Reaching.
      I'm going   to report   sniper fire.
                        Clink   clank   tink   clink   clank   tink.

Just a rock. A Corporal unwilling to ascend
the stairs of my post.
                        Never abandon your post.   Now,
I have a story   about skipping lunch,
discovering glass shielding me was plexi.
I guard the gate,   unflanked.
I am not assailed, though my body
disagrees. My joints tighten like tendons.
I sit somewhere between
trauma and a prank, pondering
exactly what I am supposed to fear.

Taps

Bugle blasts carry notes, bodies, soldier's gone down
below. Boots off. Rifle planted. Tags hung. Battle-

field cross constructed again. Watch Sisyphus pass,
rock crushes souls destined to suffer slightly less.

Flat bodies scooped up, carried with care. No soldier
left behind, descending between notes. The river

surrounding. Tune pulling them within. Satiate
death's lust for camaraderie. Return nightly now.

Racing in the Isle of Man Tourist Trophy

For the spectators it is death-defying
moments. The sound of swarms of unfathomable size
approaches, swells,
more ominous. For the riders
the moment is an extended metaphor with
death. Villages appear as breaths between trees,
like fighter pilots, the motorcycle riders sway. Grassy
green hills wave as racers speed, split the Glens
under tree canopy tunnels,
climb the highlands, crest Greeba Castle. Brown,
beige, and white buildings, rest beyond
stacked stone walls. Returning spectators lean back,
riders pass. Zip.   Rip.   Repeat.   Swirl
around the island. I've memorized
all thirty-seven markers across sixty kilometers,
scream down Bray Hill, twist
through the Nook, squeeze meters
into milliseconds. I always remember
astronauts knowing something will go wrong.
No need to cover closed eyes.
I envision: my death, my record breaking
run. The slightest
wiggle sends the rider over the handlebars
in superman pose—
a folk hero origin story
started on three-inch screens.
Approaching not   a tunnel, almost   a dot, a bullseye
—No, a crosshair
on the shifting horizon. The white lines spill.
Windy Corner, brandishing
death. I've memorized

every turn. Everyone speaks of the crashes
when you survive, the scars
they leave when you don't. Tear off the visor
leave bug carcasses behind. I brace for the hairpin,
the wheels still spin in slide,
even rider-less. If my death goes viral
my existence becomes infectious.
The faster I go
the slower the turns come.
The loose gravel produces grainy images,
sucks the slick tires off the asphalt
My knee scrapes the inside of the road, my body
stretches across the bike, pushes the wheels
apart, my face jets   an inch above
the pavement—really, I lean into the road,
assist gravity in grounding
the bike. The last dying
rider didn't die on the next straightaway,
he died just past it. I tumble off the bike,
replace the wheels and roll, arms
snap legs bend into vines,
hums become scrapes,
sparks spray   across my visor,   a steady stream
means less bounce, less chance of punctured
organs. Helmet smacks,
bones crack. My seventeen
minutes expire. They won't remember
me for dying from the crash,
but from the memorized image of my motionless
body sliding across the road, approaching death.

Olympus

I Cry Every Time I Drive

No screaming children someone
telling turns to unbend silence shakes
over-over anticipates every turn
round roadkill oncoming traffic feels present

one kid faces forward
invisible rear view I Spy something nellow
flowers, street lines, sunsets
I brake at brightening lights

slow merging sedans elicit explicit
project deformed descriptions on moving van
cut cars off they swing onto shoulder
don't bother don't glance

silence can't survive the entire drive
scream with engine rev not roar
long road trip stretches like legs
on dash asleep every second not spent scrolling

kids fake sleep avoiding rest stops
fast food does the only filling
unanswered questions keep eyes off roads

Evangelical Choir Director

She wasn't strict, she was
a proper Christian mother. Meaning
she did what she was told
as did those she gifted with life.

She professed encompassing
acceptance, bookmarked hymns
about everlasting love, even
choreographed recitals centered
around understanding. At home,

things were to be a certain way.
It does not matter where you
remember putting things
or what you want
to wear. Never tap your knee.
She will let your brothers
hit you when you do. Everyone
will scream at you to stop. Save
yourself the trouble, tap your
foot instead. Lightly. I remember

tapping my foot to a song
I don't know. I'm singing
center stage. The choir director waves
her hand, a wand without
the magic. I hated wearing
button-ups, buttoned
all the way up. But it turns out, buttons
were made with a purpose.
An Adam's apple
should only be visible to Eve.

She ensures shirts are pressed,
the house is always pristine,
a tidy tithing to the lord. The boys
chip in, as they should.
Never a mess
to be seen. Where
is the mess? I must be
on a witch hunt. Proper is how
good little boys behave
at the store. No jumping
in racks of dresses,
no screaming back
at the lights. As soon as I went

to college, my questions made me
the family loon. Spoon-fed
liberal agendas, which not only dissect,
but directly attack Christian propaganda.
When I tell her, I don't
want my children to suffer
the same abuse of indoctrination,
she stares at the devil I must be.

Nazarene Pastor

My father's hand
hugging my
throat. Passion
always displayed

firm. It was true. He had
left drinks in the car
before but *I would never*

speak to my father that way!
My father speaks
to me about responsibility,
while gauging how much
oxygen his teenage son's body
still grasps. He says *come on*

and even *don't you want to*
hit me when I do not
reciprocate his violence.
I throw the can away harder
than it deserves. I avoid
questions for two marriages.

Fully Fenced-in

Fluttering
behind that tree.   Reflections
from another era. Judgement

errors carve the scars into me.
Initials encased in hearts. Sticky
notes scatter thoughts, adhere moments of me.

The canopy sways. Light from stars dies in
branches. Spacewalks always occur inside.
Constellation crosswalks,
impeding celestial traffic.
Lunar face leers on, fully
phased. Swirling lines
do Double-Dutch upon
swimming pool surface.
A leaf jumps right in.

I Know Something

I'm not self-centered but,
I did think Rancid was singing
a song about my hometown,
until I was 33. Turns out
it was about a bomb. One that started
fusing the second I corporealized
an explosion. I escape every four years,

when I move to another suburb,
with another set of reasons
to despise what I'm meant
to become. I frame the world
with the ridges of my expertise,
and nothing an inch outside it.
A wall decoration, oft stacked
in a box. I stare at the mirror
trying to ignore my reflection.

The glass sounds like the wind—
steady, soft breeze—whistling
a wooshy tale. Remembering when
the mountains spoke more than the men
carrying rifles. The radio doesn't click.
There isn't a dial. Only buttons.
The host, named after my past,
plays a song which catches my eye.

Eternally Ephemeral

I use my fourth or fifth copy of the *Iliad*
to take notes in logistics class,
the second book a study guide.
I know everything. I am aware
          of a fraction of nothing.
The boats were stacked with lineage,
the only battles avoided through
ancestors, invoked before the spear.

I feel like a poetic form
somewhere between villanelle and sestina
          disappeared quite recently,
literally vanished. No trace,
no tangible thought. Just the idea
the structure was there. It was
established, now there is
          only   space.

          Not blankness. Unseen, stored
data. Unrouteable. Derouted.
Somehow still   plugged in.
I hate reading the *Iliad*
digitally. It speaks more
          osmotically to me. I'm
resting,   I'm what's the word   which
means enduring/rhymes with funeral?

53

ALY ALLEN

I Miney-Moed Every Major Decision

Déjà vu is not meant for
me. Intertwined reality.
Repeating what has not
happened. Iterations of ideas
so perfect though, they must have
occurred before. This
cannot be the first time.
We must always remain in
the midst. Embracing
either extreme and how their ends weave.

If I had chosen another
toe, perhaps I'd be living
coastally, still soaking, still seeping,
drinking and not yet weeping.

Never made it out onto or into
the ocean. It's not the sharks,
it's the vastness, the endless liminal
swaying, the pitch, the fear of turning
around and suddenly seeing.

Buying Gas with Quarters

I watch as the sun set behind
turns clouds cotton,
taffy—peaching pink.
Passed swaths of green—
uncut, unkempt, peripheral—
fields fluttering orange and brown,
flank the highway, a line

connects horizons. Journey
a nuisance. Who would wish
to linger within limits? Global
Positioning System reads road signs
before I make them out,
reminds me about upcoming direction.

Where I am becomes where I am lost.

No turn lanes, no-passing zones, no flow to traffic.
Headlights tuck
into my bumper,
urge the speedometer,
& the shoulder drops off,
ravine stretches down
as far as road does out.
What escape is there except forward?
Toll roads are always the preferred route.
Away from the moment,

I cross inviting intersections,
Main Streets, and speed traps.
The right of way yields.
For a moment I question

if I'm driving on the same road
as before. The GPS drowns,
bubbles just below eardrums. Beats

stretch the lines of light
like astigmatism diamonds. I drift,
merge headlights oncoming.

Where Milk Costs More Than Gas

Ding! The low fuel icon
means twenty-seven miles to empty,
we've always made it before,
on fumes more than full tanks.
Twenty-six miles to my apartment.
Usually, I'd take Fairgrounds Road
& risk the seven stop signs,
but the kids are with me,
can't / better not risk dying before the lake.
Their mom would never find us on a back road.
No. Better
head up Perkins run out: at a red light,
where kids in cars around us watch iPads.
in a crowded department-store parking lot,
where people try to find enough space
in their trunk for just three more bags.
or even next to a pump at OnCue.

We have sticky nickels,
but carrying two children inside
to buy fifty cents of fuel is the same
as asking the cashier
if they'll spot me a tank. I'd rather
run dry on country roads, even
ask their mother again for help.
She can be our gas station savior,
we'll play eye-spy-with-my-little-eyes,
until she arrives. The kids' mom,
I never call her ex-wife, lives
just far enough away to rely on.
We'll just keep driving along
the way she knows how to help.

ALY ALLEN

[ˈmaskyələn]

I walk down a dark street
hollering. A man, well outside arms-reach,
hears me,
looks up,
crosses the street.
My voice is baritone, my beard is unkempt.
Neither are my fault. I shout,
You! Yeah, you. Come
back over here. He hesitates,
shuffles across the unlit
road, his head
begging his feet to turn. *Were you*
avoiding me? He nods. *Afraid*
I was going to do something?
He nods
once. *Fuckin' hurt you?* He stands
frigid. His bangs sway. *I wouldn't.*
He peeks,
I'm gentle.
down the street behind
me. *You can go.*
He sprints out of earshot. I scream
regardless,   *Remember,*
I ain't fuckin' scary.
You aren't fuckin' scared.
He doesn't hear me, but I do.

Good Dad,

Bad Mom

Buys lots of presents.
Works too much.
Hires a babysitter.
Allows the kids to run.

Doesn't worry.
Parties on the weekend.
Calls a sober driver.
Apologizes for mistakes.

Outside, at home, in the store.
Not visibly abusing.
They holler in the store,
Encouraging creativity,
misbehaving in public.
Strangers approve aloud,

There is no nuance.
Indulgent with self-care.
disappear into the middle.
disrupting clothing racks,
Mirror displaying mirror.
provide a singular reflection.

ALY ALLEN

Tinnitus

Starts with a hand cupped
Slapping the side of your
Head covering your ear
Sending the vibration
Drumming umming umming

Mansplainer

He didn't mean it
that way. He spoke out
of context. He had nothing
discriminatory in mind. Smiled
because he was uncomfortable. Insulted
them on accident. Initiated
the problem. Yes. He
really is a conflict
resolution specialist. He isn't
looking for trouble. Gets it,
the last word, every time
there's an argument. He doesn't know
how to process emotions. Through violence
finds some peace, takes it
from others. Assumes they want him
to have it. Lacks understanding. Someone else
explains.   Isn't alright with himself.
She knows more than him
about everything, except
this. He says the same thing
three different ways. Telling her
the point at which to start a circle.

I Know Sisyphus

You've got it all wrong
I don't know whether they love
Their stone or rolling it more.
Their stone
Or rolling it more
They love
Whether
I don't
Know you've got it
All wrong
I know the roll of Sisyphus' stone
I know the song it squeezes
From the hillside

Grounding

There is a pile of avocados. They are
not hand grenades. Those watermelons
are striped, not wired. The inflatable
football field, atop the frozen food isle,
is ineffective cover. The grocer stocking
the bananas looks as annoyed
as I am, there is barely a speck of yellow

in a field of phallic green. The handle for
the cart is moist. I hope I've
been sweating. My leggings
are thin and cool today. They feel
like my insides when I'm hugged
by someone I didn't know
loved me. My hair is
tangled on the left. I'm sure
I look vain, running both
hands through it. The pineapple
is heavier than I expected. The frond
plucks right out. The automatic
doors are not helicopter
blades, they only opened

three times. The manager is explaining
why the new cashier needs to arrive
early not just on time. The lights
buzz low, or maybe
the fixtures are just higher
in here. The prepackaged
cookies open with that plastic
pop. I'm glad the medical mask

keeps my breath from everyone
around me. I finished all
the coffee this morning. It's half
the reason we are here. The other
are those cakes, that warm baked flour,
wafting into everyone.
Biting my cheek, the metallic
tint allows me to begin again.

The Air is Different

Ever since they were
Alive my first-born
Has been soothed by the sky.

Named after the stars,
They scream under roof.

As soon as the screen
Door opens, the
Steam rushes out,
The cool air overflows,

The wonder overwhelms.

No whimper, no wailing,
Slow steady breaths,
Not a single request.

Hero Worship

Writing Poems

The truth is there
below, between, among
the words. Sometimes leap
ahead of the sentence.
Seeking meaning in the ending
when we need
entanglement of everything.

ALY ALLEN

Gallery Debut

Enter a glowing room—
It only burns my fingers
when unscrewing the first few
bulbs. Held by artists, parents,
examples. I twist, unwind, & darken
the room, interrupting the current.
My light eclipses, reestablishes

my periphery. I could have switched them off,
instead, I unscrewed them.
Turn my own in
their place. Use black
lights, display my path.

Lecture Notebooks

Filled with doodles
more sketches than letters
the notes aren't buried
they are the background

the images I already know
erupt pour out
flood sentences with color

ALY ALLEN

Where has it Gone?

It was just here // just had it // was in
the other room // no not this one //
couldn't have set it // didn't
throw it out // was thinking about//
was looking at the counter // no, nothing
on the counter // when did I realize
it escaped // where did we start // where
was I standing // what angle did I peek //
went from coffee pot
to trash can // my mind was
leaping from old friends and
old places // masks of me // thresholds
keep seizing memories // every
room // anew // a new idea // trace
my steps // lost
when I looked at my phone //
turn it off // back on // power
off // sit still // start new
thoughts // in media res of the missing

If you try and Squeeze

Another thought
in, you will lose
the one you meant
to write down

and miss the part
where you turn it
into an idea.
Draw from the ether
And sketch with sweat.

ALY ALLEN

Actively Lethargic

Charging for the couch
Sprinting through the outside
Mud-like muck-like
Motivation thickens
Scrolling, swiping, sighting
Within within
With in
Wi thin
Why the inn
Well within

I Go to the Coffee House to Write

I have a lot of redeeming qualities,
Which means I'm tolerable.
I make my presence
bearable in moments. I distract
well from the reality of me. The first
few chews of Dubble Bubble.

I am pretty sure Tootsie Rolls multiply
if you let them rest long enough
underneath other Halloween candy.

I don't write with my quill,
but I mention it casually
during workshop.

On Tuesdays, I bring
a chisel & slab.
I order something seasonal
& I began to notch.
I hoard every shard,
every chip, as I imagine
other patrons yearning to collect
unseen letters—
the rubble of the soon to be spoken.

Sometimes a Poem

is a moment. No
matter the changes
they never feel
correct. The original
entrenches. Other times

a poem sings
in the direction
of the unsought
truth. The ring
'round an anchored
word, prolongs departure.

Meaning, the crew
untangle the rope—
untether the dock—
unclock the watch—
sail into storms,
prepare to float
upon shattered bits
of ship. Raindrops
spot the sea's
surface with synchronicity,
singing, echoing, locating.

The Molecules in Water Begin Vibrating

When I speak, I sound
like I'm seeking appraisal.

When I sigh, I signal
I'm seething. Tea kettle

when I shout. I show you
I'm soothing myself. When

I whisper, *I want you*
I'm staring at stainless steel.

Writer's Block

If you could
      give me a deadline
            I'd have a great starting point.
Also, this will be late,
      it's the opposite of the army,
            where 15-minutes-early is on-time.
               Three-days-late is early.
It's not the pressure I need,
      not the expectation.
            I have to know you are
               disappointed, that your
                  perception has reset.

Chaos Makes me Shimmer, Glimmer at the Proper Angle

I do not water my own
Plants. I spend
All energy subverting
Myself. The world needs
To see a certain glitter-free aesthetic,
Stoic, statuesque Midas—centuries spent
Still in the corner. Polished thrice
Before any visitor's arrival. I check
My posture in the outer circle
Of their eye. Draped in vines,
Blossomed flowers, and of course
Poison oak. It's not the shimmer
That's fake, it's the seasonal
Nature of it. The opposite of

Gilded, I'm all gold inside.
It's possible to plant now
To pot the life once meant
To grow without the aid of bulbs.

Acknowledgements

I am grateful to the editors of the following magazines and journals, in which these poems first appeared—some in slightly different versions:

"Buying Gas with Quarters" originally appeared in *Kelp Journal: The Wave*, April 2023

"Culpability" originally appeared in an anthology titled *The Poppy: A Symbol of Remembrance*, Southern Arizona Press, September 2022

"Grounding" originally appeared in *Apocalypse Confidentia,* as part of a special themed presentation on "War," November 2022

"Fort Drum, 2008" originally appeared in the *Line of Advance* literary journal, March 2023

"I Know Sisyphus" originally appeared in *Press Pause*, June 2019

"I Miney-Moed Every Major Decision" originally appeared in *Kelp Journal: The Wave*, April 2023

['maskyələn] originally appeared in *Two Hawks Quarterly*, Spring 2023

"Plead for me Thetis" originally appeared in *Carmina Magazine*, September 2022

"Portrait in Apocalypse" originally appeared in *Glass Mountain,* Fall 2019. The poem was awarded the Lillie Robertson Prize for poetry at the 2019 Boldface Conference at the University of Houston.

"Racing in the Isle of Man Tourist Trophy" originally appeared in *New Note Poetry*, Winter 2022-2023

"Roll Call" originally appeared in *As You Were*, the literary journal of Military Experience & the Arts, November 2022

In addition to the above, the following poems also appeared in the chapbook *Approaching Valhalla,* published in 2022 by Bottlecap Press: "Plead for me Thetis," "Road Trip," "Guard Tower," "Taps," "From Behind Me," "Restless-leg Syndrome," "Listen up Kids," "Battle Buddy," "I Stepped on Legos to Prepare for This Poem: A Triptych," "Roll Call," "Evangelical Choir Director," "Fully Fenced-in," "I Keep Putting the Baby Gate Back up," "Eternally Ephemeral," and each of the three poems titled "Tinnitus."

Glossary

Black Hawk: The UH-60 "Black Hawk" utility helicopter is a four-blade, twin-engine, medium-lift manufactured by Sikorsky Aircraft. It can transport up to 11 troops with equipment.

G.P.S.: Global Positioning System

"Grounding": The poem of this title refers to a 5-4-3-2-1 sensory exercise for self-soothing during periods of anxiety or stress.

I.E.D. Improvised Explosive Device. A "homemade" bomb or mine constructed of parts, including military scrap or surplus, not originally intended for such use.

M4: The M16 ("em-sixteen") family of semi-automatic assault rifles has been issued to U.S. Army soldiers since 1969. It fires a 5.56mm round, usually as either single shots or three-round "bursts." A shorter version, the M4 carbine, gradually replaced the M16 rifle starting in 1994.

"Eeny, Meeny, Miny, Moe" is a children's counting rhyme.

OKC: The three-letter location identifier for Will Rogers World Airport, Oklahoma City, Oklahoma, as designated by the International Air Transport Association (IATA).

OnCue: A family-owned regional chain of convenience stores, headquartered in Stillwater, Oklahoma.

Rancid: An American punk rock band founded in 1991. Anecdotally, a few denizens of Tomball, Texas mistakenly thought they heard the town referenced in the band's highest-charting single, "Time Bomb."

Under Armour: A U.S. manufacturer of athletic footwear and apparel headquartered in Baltimore, Maryland.

A Few Words of Thanks

Endless gratitude to my writing instructors, advisors, and mentors over the years for their time, expertise, but most of all their ideas: Melissa Studdard, Niki Herd, Kevin Prufer, Nick Flynn, Janine Joseph, Lisa Lewis.

Thank you to my classmates, contemporaries, committee members, and friends along the way for their feedback on many of these poems, especially: Aris Kian, Roseanna Recchia, Remi Recchia, Whitney Koo, Jenn Conner, Chrissy Martin, Dani Putney, Caleb Jordan, Jen Hudgens, Caleigh Shaw, Brianne Grothe, Autumn Schraufnagel, Katie McMorris, Allyn Bernkopf, April Lim, Saga Walls, John Andrews, and Laura Minor.

Thank you to my parents.

Thank you, Ari, for always telling me to keep writing and to cease miming.

Thanks to my fellow war poets: U.S. Army veteran Jason Poudrier (*Red Fields*); U.S. Marine Corps spouse Lisa Stice (*FORCES*; *Permanent Change of Station*; *Uniform*; and more); U.S. Army veteran Jessi M. Atherton (*The Time War Takes*); U.S. Army veteran Randy Brown (*Welcome to FOB Haiku*); and fellow Oklahoma poet Gary Reddin (*An Abridged History of American Violence* and *Quantum Entanglement*) for their insights and early endorsements of this collection.

Finally, and mostly, thank you, H. and S.—and to their mom and her partner—for the time, energy, patience, flexibility, love, encouragement, inspiration, and for continually expanding my heart and mind.

Artist's Statement

This collection comprises poems focused on the deconstruction and reconstruction of the self, but also the relationship between self and others. Topics include Post-Traumatic Stress Disorder (PTSD), suicide, intrusive thoughts, intergenerational trauma, and most importantly, hope for growth.

The poems work together to locate internalized violence and to repurpose it for something positive, but also to sever the toxic ties of intergenerational trauma. Individually, the poems deal with uncovering societal truths (acceptance and glorification of violence) and unmasking the self (internalized violence and trauma). We must be aware not only of the wounds we inherit, but those we inflict.

Soldiers often utter the phrase "Until Valhalla" when addressing a fellow warrior who fell in battle. It is also passed among living warriors, an incantation of mutual regard and devotion—and an implication, in some ways, that at least one will likely fall on the battlefield, or someday succumb to battle wounds.

In Nordic mythology, the great hall in Asgard is a location in the afterlife, one specifically designated for those slain in combat. There, fallen warriors drink and dine excessively between war games, training and preparing for Ragnarök, a climactic end-of-the-world battle that we humans are destined to lose. On this side of existence, the promise of such an inconvenient fate does nothing to dissuade our fervor: We often wish to return to battle in the company of those we have lost. The resulting dissonance can echo across lives, or even between generations. Survivor's guilt can motivate many self-destructive behaviors.

I titled my first chapbook "Approaching Valhalla." At this point in my own life's journey, however, I now seek to avoid that mythological reunion. How better to fling the frailty of life into the faces of unseen Gods, after all, than to continue living and growing?

—Aly Allen

About the Author

Aly Allen is a neurodivergent parent and Operational Enduring Freedom (OEF) veteran diagnosed with Post-Traumatic Stress Disorder (PTSD). Her kids are also neurodivergent. She served in the U.S. Army as a broadcast journalist for five years, deploying to Afghanistan once with the U.S. 10th Mountain Division. Aly recently began gender-transition, after years of sobriety and therapy.

After separating from the military, Aly resumed college to be a professor and a writer. She met her first wife, had two kids, and they got divorced. Her writing often ponders the effects war has on her children and first wife. Soldiers and veterans are directly affected by their time in service, she says, but how many others inherit these wounds?

Many of Aly's poems thrust readers into the midst of daily chaos—whether in the parental or soldierly gaze—weaving attempts to navigate parent-child relationships both present and past, wrestling with grief and guilt, but also growing in hope toward stability and healing.

Aly's 2022 chapbook *Approaching Valhalla* is available from Bottlecap Press. Her poetry and creative non-fiction have appeared in venues such as *Consequence, Carmina Magazine, Apocalypse Confidential, Press Pause, New Note,* and elsewhere.

Aly earned a bachelor of arts in creative writing from University of Houston, and a Master of Fine Arts in creative writing from Oklahoma State University, Stillwater, where she now teaches composition.

Empowered by a grant from Oklahoma State University's Edmon Low Library, she founded the Military Memoirs Writing Workshop. The program pairs members of the military-connected community with graduate students in the English and Counseling departments, centering the idea of writing as catharsis. The program has already produced a chapbook of poems and fiction, co-authored by a veteran and their daughter.

Also from Middle West Press LLC

anthology

Our Best War Stories:
Prize-winning Poetry & Prose
from the Col. Darron L. Wright Memorial Awards
Edited by Christopher Lyke

poetry collections

Hugging This Rock: Poems of Earth & Sky, Love & War
by Eric Chandler

Permanent Change of Station and *FORCES*
by Lisa Stice

Always Ready: Poems from a Life in the U.S. Coast Guard
by Benjamin B. White

September Eleventh: an epic poem, in fragments
by Amalie Flynn

Blood / Not Blood, Then the Gates
by Ron Riekki

HEAT + PRESSURE: Poems from War
by Ben Weakley

Welcome to FOB Haiku:
War Poems from Inside the Wire
by Randy Brown, a.k.a. "Charlie Sherpa"

Made in the USA
Columbia, SC
17 October 2023

24223915R00057